Joseph Marchese

The Handbook of a Successful Salesperson

Handbook / Notebook / Day Planner

Dedication

I AM DEDICATING THIS BOOK TO all the hardworking salespeople that love their job in sales but need some guidance or just want to be better at what they do EVERYDAY. I do not know everything about sales; I feel no one does. I have succeeded in sales, and I have failed in sales. This Handbook/Workbook is a compilation of my knowledge and experience to help people make sense of an ever-changing lucrative environment and give an order to some already known as well as new processes.

If you are brand new in sales or you've been selling for years, you'll fine value in this tool.

Remember, you have chosen a career that you have full control for your success as well as your failure. Take time EVERY day to learn something new. The ever-changing environment of sales requires you to be able to conform to any situation. You have made the first step of many in bettering yourself by purchasing this book. Now learn from it and take it to the field!

Best of luck in your journey!

TABLE OF CONTENTS

INTRODUCTION

WHETHER YOU ARE JUST STARTING OUT IN SALES or a seasoned salesperson, this handbook will guide you in being a successful salesperson. Let me explain. First things first, you have to understand that sales is psychological. Good days in sales and bad days in sales all stem from your mindset. Keep this statement in mind while reading through the chapters. When you enjoy and understand the product or service that you are selling, it becomes fun! If you're having fun, you'll learn above and beyond "just the basics" of the value you can bring to a customer. In turn, differentiate yourself from all the other salespeople that are banging on YOUR customers doors. In this handbook, you will learn secrets that I have completed over my 29-year sales career. I will warn you up front, this handbook is filled with golden nuggets that you will want to start executing on immediately. Whether you are just starting out in sales or have been at it for years, my advice is, slowly weave in these concepts. Take baby steps and perfect what you see as valuable. I did not write this to change everything you are doing; you already have talent, and probably know about lots of the things that I talk about in this handbook. I simply want to organize your process and add more tools to your tool bag to build an even bigger and better foundation that you may already have. Share as much as you choose to with other salespeople. As you will read in my handbook, becoming a mentor of sales will only make you better at selling. As you begin to read, I promise you will begin to develop a more positive and success-driven attitude, simply because lots of the concepts that I wrote about spawn from sales common sense (you most likely already have this!). A person with a sales mindset will begin to feel anxious while reading many of my words; the reason is, you will most likely be familiar with the concepts, but will become excited that someone has given them an order for you to follow. Using technology in sales today is also spoken about in this handbook. You will learn some new communication techniques; do not be afraid of them and embrace them. The world of sales changes every day; you must be that salesperson that conforms and changes with the times. This is a great handbook to keep close to you as a reference and refer to before you enter a meeting with a customer. Use it anyway you want, just be open-minded to learning new skills or polish your existing skills. Enjoy the read and spread the knowledge.

CHAPTER ONE

Where Do You Start?

THE BEAUTY OF A SALES CAREER is whether you're a high school grad, college grad, or just looking to make a change, sales could be for you! Many colleges, no matter what the profession is that you studied, tell their students to look for a job in sales before you settle down in a job you went to school for. They understand that the experience and "street smarts" that you will gain by doing this is priceless. Over the years, I have had the pleasure of meeting thousands of sales professionals in many different times of their careers. Some just starting out and some that have been at it for years. The number 1 piece of advice that everyone gave me was "love what you do every day." I never took this advice lightly. Now I am telling you the same thing.

But first, where do you start? How do you differentiate yourself with your resume? How do you handle yourself in an interview?

Let us jump in . . .

Your resume

I have seen and reviewed LOTS of resumes.

The commonality amongst most is just lots of words on a sheet of paper. The interviewer or recruiter will start to read your well-thought-out explanation of your previous positions and/or experience. As they glance down, they see some key words they are looking for, and you might get a call. They review so many resumes.

What if you added some excitement to help advertise yourself? With today's technology, I am shocked we still write boring resumes that are just full of words.

Get creative! Obviously keeping it professional. Here are some tips!

1.   Create an intro video: There are so many ways to do this. Record yourself with your phone or computer cam. Keep it short and to the point. Dress properly for the role. And catch their attention with some unique information about yourself. * Scan this QR code below to see an example.

2.   Create a QR code: Once you recorded that attention-catching video, now it is time to QR code it! There are numerous free apps and programs that can help you do this. * Here is an example,

QR code example of Intro video for resume

Scan this ----

3.   Add some previous company logos or the college logo. However you want to position it, add the pictures of these logos on your resume. Instead of the reviewer just having to read about your past experiences, let the expen-

sive logo that these companies paid lots of money for be the familiarity that your reviewer recognizes.

4. Consider your resume a "living document." Many people construct a resume when it is time to look for a new job. Take the time EVERY month to add some experience to your resume. Instead of trying to think back of all your accomplishments, add it when those milestones happen. This way, when and if a new opportunity presents itself, you'll have a "rock solid" resume to rely on to paint the best picture possible of what you can bring to the table!

I know some of these tips might seem out of the ordinary. But that is exactly what you're trying to do! Stay professional!! But be different. I promise it is worth a try!

You landed an interview!

Congratulations! Your innovative resume has caught someone's attention! Now what?

Maybe you received a call, maybe you got an email, whatever the case, they are interested in a first conversation!

Let us review. In today's world a remote online interview is not out of the question. No matter what anyone tells you, make sure you wear pants for this conversation! 😄 Also, just be prepared for that in-person interview as well.

Here are 10 tips I do to prepare for and attend an interview.

1. Reread the job description. If you can, print it out so you have it in front of you for the interview. Highlight the areas you have experience in, and jot down some notes to help you articulate your value in these areas.

2. Research the company! Understand key information about the company you are interviewing with. Especially gather as much sales information as you can. This will give you insight and confidence to speak professionally about how your background makes you a great fit! Use the company website and social media to aid you in this process.

3. Prepare great questions! Interviewers expect questions. So instead of just coming up with some on the fly, prepare some great questions. Here are a few that I have used.

> 1) Can you tell me some of the day-to-day responsibilities of a salesperson in this role?
>
> 2) How is my performance measured?
>
> 3) What are some of the challenge's salespeople face in this role?

4. (If face to face) Plan your schedule so you can arrive 10–15 min early. Do a "dry run" to the location and learn the surroundings, so you know where to park and how long it should take you to get there. With the extra time you planed, while waiting for your interviewer, get a feel for the environment and dynamics in the office.

5. Practice body language. Sit or stand tall! You made it to the interview desk! Be proud and show it. Remember, they are looking at you in the eyes of one of their customers. Take a deep breath to manage any feelings of anxiety. Look the person in the eye and give them a firm handshake! Without crushing their hand of course. 😂

6. Win them over with your positivity and truthfulness. Stay positive about all your past experiences; never speak negatively about current and past employers. While it can seem tempting to embellish on your skills and accomplishments, interviewers find honesty refreshing and respectable. But remember, there is a fine line between being confident and coming across as cocky.

7. Bring a note pad and do not be afraid to use their white board. Obviously, the notepad is for you to take notes. But, quick story, I remember when I was in an interview and the opportunity presented itself for me to explain something I had to write to explain, so I got up from my chair and wrote on the interviewer's white board, and before I knew it, the person was standing up next to me fully interested in what I was explaining and writing. I got that job . . . and the interviewer told me that they were impressed on how I used the whiteboard to explain. If a whiteboard is not available, use your notepad!

8. Salary Expectations: This is an important one. How many times have you had an interview and the person behind the desk asked you, "What are your salary expectations?" This question MUST be handled in a certain way. If this question is asked in your very first interview, most likely the interviewer is looking to weed out people that have high expectations that cannot be offered by that company; in turn, they are dwindling the applicant list down by asking this question. The best way to handle this question is to simply say, "I would have to hear more about the position and my day-to-day responsibilities to answer that correctly." Try to avoid giving that number away until you absolutely must answer it. I know this isn't always easy, but do the best you can.

9. What happens next? It is perfectly acceptable to ask about next steps in the process. Remember, as a sales professional, you will be doing this with your customer so the interviewer might be looking for you to do this.

10. Send a personalized thank you. Make sure you have the correct information of the interviewer and if anyone else was present. Remember you are trying to make an impression, so a traditional thank you card written by you is a great idea, but don't forget all that technology that's available to you. A thank you video will definitely differentiate you! See example,

QR code example of a thank you video after an interview.

Scan this -----

Keeping all these golden nuggets in mind, remember, interviews for a sales position are set up to see how you present as a candidate that will be front facing to this company's customers. They want you to represent professionalism, knowledge, and bring business expertise. If you show none of these attributes, the interviewer will be promoted to keep looking.

Notes you want to remember from this chapter.

_____

_____

_____

_____

_____

_____

_____

_____

_____

_____

_____

_____

_____

_____

_____

_____

_____

_____

_____

_____

_____

_____

CHAPTER TWO

You Got the Job!! (Early preparation to starting my new job in sales)

LET'S FACE IT, STARTING ANY NEW JOB CAN BE EXCITING. But with that excitement comes lots of uncertainty. Starting a job in sales also comes with its own set of concerns. Learning the products and services, what my territory will look like, will I mesh well with the other salespeople on the team, I could go on ... As I mentioned earlier, psychologically being prepared is the number 1 thing you must focus on.

No worries, the things I mentioned above will fall into place, but let us talk about your mindset.

As a salesperson, you must be hungry. And I do not mean starving yourself and not eating that Italian sub you love; what I mean when I say hungry is, you must be that sales rep that wakes up early, has your day prepared in advance, has laid out clothes for the day the night before, and has goals for each and every day. For example, if I had a certain add-on product that could enhance my sales, I would set a goal to make sure anyone I spoke to that day would know about that add-on product. Or let's say you told yourself as a goal today I want to introduce myself to 10 new people and let them know what you do for a living and maybe connect with them on a professional social media platform.

Whatever your goals are, they must revolve around moving you forward and achieving your sales goals. When you set goals and achieve them or even come close to achieving them, your mindset becomes positive and the more you will set goals to achieve! And let's face it, if you start to do this every day, the outcome will be much better than if you do nothing at all.

Let us not forget about your personal goals as well. But I will say, through my years of sales, when you hit your professional goals, your personal goals become a lot easier to achieve. So, it's all about mindset!

A sales manager will be looking for you to be coachable and organized with the information they provide you. Take the time to prepare to hit the ground running properly. It will be tempting to just get in the field and start selling, but take the time to understand your new role and all the value your new company offers its customers. The best analogy I can come up with is, it is like going on a hunting trip and leaving the ammunition at home. Do not be that rep. I promise you will miss opportunities just because you don't understand fully what your new company can offer and the business pains it can solve.

A certain amount of failure in sales is inevitable, and it has an impact on your mindset. Be patient; the best thing to do to avoid failure is follow the onboarding process your company has laid out for you, learn as much as you can, and take advantage of the time given that you are not expected to generate revenue while you're still green in your new job.

Success is infectious, and it really does put a fire under a salesperson's actions. But like I just said, failure can have an extremely negative impact as well.

So, here are some tips on what to focus on during your onboarding process.

1.   Learn as much as possible about the product or service you will be offering. Write down all the value propositions and the business pains they can

solve. GOLDEN NUGGET—when you first start in the field, it's ok to have this list in front of you on a sales call to refer to.

2. Learn as much as possible about the company CRM (customer relationship management program). Typically, these programs will allow you to organize your territory and have your specific customer base loaded in for you to manage. In a lot of situations, you are going to be taking over a previously owned territory. So most importantly, manage your "low hanging fruit." Get in front of existing customers that are already doing business with your company and introduce yourself. Look for customers that may have gone dormant. Lots of times customers stop doing business with a company because the last rep was not attentive enough to their needs. Revitalize your dormant customers! You are the new rep in town; get your name out there! If possible, organize your territory, so you can cover and travel the whole area effectively in a one-week time frame, Monday through Friday. This way, your customer base gets used to when they might be seeing you. And more importantly, you familiarize yourself with the landscape. This also helps you optimize your schedule when making prospecting phone calls.

3. Shadowing: Take the initiative! If your company does not have a plan in place already to schedule some time for you to shadow other employees, I suggest you do so. Spend time with the people that will help you achieve success! As a sales rep, you will have to interact with other employees to help your sales process and most importantly for the customer to have a seamless transaction with your company. Come up with some good questions to ask during this shadowing time, for example:

A. What are the main responsibilities of the person in this job role?

B. How will this person interact with you?

C. What can you do to make this person's job easier?

D. How does this person's role effect your job responsibilities?

E. If you had to step into this person's role, could you perform their job responsibilities?

When you take the time to learn what other people do, that effects your performance; you can understand what THEY NEED to help you achieve your goals. Remember mindset, solid business, and personal relationships are important to have. Celebrate their achievements as well as yours. Helping one another achieve business goals creates a healthy culture. Now, I am not saying they must attend your child's birthday party on the weekend, but develop a relationship where that might not be out of the question. When a company adapts to this type of culture, the whole organization benefits!

4. Compile existing customer feedback.

This one was big for me. When I first started, I was very inquisitive about what our good customers liked about doing business with the company. It is important to find out why a customer chooses to do business with a particular company and use these success stories to gain more business! If you find out that an existing customer solved a business challenge with a certain value proposition your company offers, the next time you are in a meeting and that customer presents the same challenge, you can share with them how you were able to help another customer with that exact business pain. This is called Business Expertise! The majority of sales calls fail due to the fact that the salesperson brings NO business expertise to the table. Salespeople tend to resort to trying to build rapport with weekend game stats and hunting stories when little do they know, the customer wants to trust a vendor more than know someone that can update them on who won the big game this weekend! Bring some business expertise to your conversations, and THEN once a business relationship has grown, then it is time to talk about the fun stuff. This is a HUGE differentiator! And that's when long lasting business relationships are built and give you and your company credibility and stability.

5. Set attainable goals.

Every new salesperson, when they start a new job, is excited to show what they can bring to the table. If you are a competitive person, like I am, you will have to be incredibly careful of this. Every company allows for "ramp-up time." Take advantage of this time and implement the steps you are reading about in my handbook. Take baby steps but set attainable goals EVERY week that you can achieve. Goals are so important, but one thing to remember about goals is if you are the only one that knows about them, sometimes they are harder to hit. Let me explain, when I first started out, I made sure other people knew what I was trying to achieve, like my significant other, my best friend, and of course, my boss. Why did I do this you ask? Well, when other people are involved, they will cheer you on, they will keep you in check and ask how you're doing midweek, and you will not want to disappoint them. In turn, you will make it more of a point to hit those goals. Remember, sales is psychological! I worked for a company once that would call my wife and let her know where I stood in a contest that if I won, would take her to the Caribbean Islands! So, you can be sure she would ask me about my progress in the contest EVERY WEEK! I won that contest, and we had an awesome time!! Involve other people and crush your goals.

6. Tell EVERYONE you know about your new job.

This is important, especially in sales. Success in sales revolves around networking. We will cover that later in the handbook. The more people who know what you do, the better your chances will be of succeeding. In one of my previous roles, part of my job was to sell used construction equipment. This is a commodity that almost anyone will know someone that I could sell to. I focused and set goals as a part of everyday routine, concentrating my energy on this part of the business. My success was evident in my paychecks. Letting everyone you know and posting on business social media platforms is a good way to "advertise" yourself and what you do! Be proactive and get creative. Like I spoke about in the previous sections, maybe make a video of yourself and what you offer. This can be used in many ways. Attach the video to your email signature, assign a QR code to this video and get it put on your business card, do an email to a targeted audience and attach your video or QR code. * SEE QR code sample coming up on page 25.

Notes you will want to remember from this chapter

_____

_____

_____

_____

_____

_____

_____

_____

_____

_____

_____

_____

_____

_____

_____

_____

_____

_____

_____

_____

_____

_____

_____

_____

_____

_____

CHAPTER THREE

Field Preparation

OK, SO YOU HAVE BEEN IN YOUR ROLE FOR A FEW WEEKS, and you have followed the direction that I have laid out for you to follow. Now, it is time to start preparing your weeks to be as productive as possible. Quick reminder, in a sales role, your success is TOTALLY UP TO YOU! So, you want to make sure you plan out, at least a week in advance, what your activity will consist of daily. The less you have planned on your schedule, the less potential you have to make money. The MORE you have on your schedule, the more potential you will have to crush it and hit your goals! But the meetings must be PLANED! I will explain,

Personally, I'm a HUGE fan of planed meetings; what this means is that YOU and THE CUSTOMER have a planned time to meet and you have a chance to execute a sales process from beginning to end. I can't tell you how many times in my training classes I would ask, "OK, how many of you have meetings that are set up on your schedule for next week?" Literally everyone in the class would raise their hands. But when I dug a little deeper and said, "OK, how many of those meetings know you're coming and have planned time aside to sit with you?" Only about a quarter of the people raised their hand back up. Basically, what many salespeople do is fill their schedule with "stop-byes" and hope to obtain a meeting on the fly. My opinion about "stop-byes" is they can be a waste of time. Especially in today's world. Now do not get me wrong; if you have a robust week planned with lots of planned meetings, then sprinkling stop byes in is a smart move. Just do not depend on them for solid conversations.

Part of a GREAT schedule consists of planning time to make prospecting phone calls. You must have time planned to do this, or it will never happen. My suggestion is consistent small time slots, approximately two-hour time slots three times a week, the same time every week to hammer out as many calls as possible. Remember we talked about goals? This is a great time to set some goals around how many calls you can make and what your process is to handle common obstacles like gatekeepers and objections. Your main goal on a prospecting call is to secure a sold time for an appointment. Try not to start the selling process over the phone. Keep it brief, handle the objections they have for taking a meeting, and then offer a FEW times to meet. The more information you give them on the phone about you and your products and services, the more time you will give them to decline a meeting. I mean think about that for a second, you have not even met the person yet, and you want to tell them all the great things your company offers.

You have no idea yet what business pains or interests they have yet; why would you start dumping all this information on them over the phone? We will be talking about this more in the upcoming sections, but you must find out by asking great questions revolving around how you can really help them, and the appropriate time to do that is when you are face to face in a planned meeting. I know it is exciting that you have so many solutions that your company offers but STOP throwing up all over the phone before you know what the customer really needs and what problems you can solve. Set a PLANED meeting!

Let's talk quickly about how long meetings should take. Now depending on your industry, meetings could take anywhere from 20 minutes to one hour. Whatever the time your industry yields for a good productive meeting, keep that amount of time in mind when scheduling your week.

Let's do a quick example:

If you know a good productive meeting takes 30 minutes, and you take some drive time (10 minute-ish) into consideration, and if you plan your week appropriately, NOT driving all over your territory, working in a concentrated area, that means each meeting, in total, should only take 40 minutes out of your day. Now, the average salesperson, IF HUNGRY, should be working around a 9–10 hours a day, that's my professional opinion. So, by using the example above, you should be able to plan at least six SOLID face-to-face meetings per day! Think about if you could meet with at least six customers per day!! That is a total of only four hours, give or take, of a 9–10-hour day! Then like we spoke about previously; you could sprinkle in any stop-byes and also have time to set aside prospecting phone calls to keep scheduling these productive weeks! Most salespeople after being in the field for many years will always challenge me on this concept, but what I find in speaking with them is they just lost the thought process around this concept over the years. Being new in your role, if you start out building your schedule with this concept in mind, and have success, you will not fall into the trap that 10-year reps do by not organizing their weeks. Let's take a look at a sample schedule.

Sample Schedule

	Monday	Tuesday	Wednesday	Thursday	Friday
8:00		Prospect Calls		Meeting ½ H	Meeting ½ H
8:30	Meeting ½ H	In the office	Meeting ½ H		
9:00				Meeting 1H	Meeting ½ H
9:30	Meeting ½ H		Meeting ½ H		
10:00					Meeting ½ H
10:30	Meeting 1H		Meeting 1H	Meeting 1H	
11:00		Meeting ½ H			3 Stop by's
11:30				1 Stop by	
12:00	Lunch ½ H	Networking Lunch 1H	Lunch ½ H	Networking Lunch 1H	Networking Lunch 1H
12:30					
1:00	2 Stop by's		2 Stop by's		
1:30		Meeting ½ H		Meeting ½ H	Meeting ½ H
2:00	Meeting ½ H		Meeting ½ H		
2:30		Meeting ½ H		Prospect Calls	Meeting ½ H
3:00	Meeting ½ H		Meeting ½ H	In the office	Office or Home
3:30		Meeting 1H			Prospect Calls
4:00	Meeting ½ H		Meeting ½ H		Sunday – Planning
4:30					Spend some time
5:00	Go Home!	2 Stop by's	Go Home!	2 stop by's	Researching your
	Go to the Gym!				Upcoming week's
		Enjoy Family!			Meetings! LinkedIn
			Enjoy a Drink!		Company CRM,
				Have Dinner!	Google search

REMEMBER: This is a sample schedule. Use the format as you see fit. But I will press upon the fact that if you **do not** schedule out your weeks in advance and have a **PLAN** for **every day** in the field, you will find it challenging to be organized, and it will cause you to feel overwhelmed.

Monday: **Six** scheduled meetings, **3 and half** hours of face-to-face meetings.

Tuesday: Prospecting call time—**four** scheduled meetings, **two and half** hours of face-to-face meetings.

Wednesday: **Six** scheduled meetings, **three and half** hours of face-to-face meetings.

Thursday: Prospecting call time—**four** scheduled meetings, **three** hours of face-to-face meetings.

Friday: Prospecting call time—**five** scheduled meetings, **two and half** hours of face-to-face meetings.

12 stop byes for the week (cold calls) depending on how the meetings go, you might be able to sprinkle in a few more cold calls as the week goes on. Play that by ear.

Now, this schedule might look overwhelming, but it only reflects **19 hours and 15 minutes (taking drive time into consideration) of face-to-face scheduled meeting time with customers out of a 45-hour work week!** What are you doing with the other 25 hours and 45 minutes each week? Think about that, you are getting a chance to schedule 25 meetings with potential customers! I want you to look yourself in the mirror and ask yourself how many SCHEDULED meetings you attend each week. Friends, this is just a sample schedule, use it as a guide, and I promise you will feel more organized and feel like you have a better direction each week.

In sales, if you think you can just hop in your vehicle and drive around your territory and customers are going to wave you down, you are very much mistaken. It's all up to you. So, take this section very seriously and make up your mind to schedule EVERY week in advance. I promise you will advance very quickly in your new sales career!

Time Blocking: Let us not forget the most important thing! Now, we just talked about how long meetings should take, knowing this information will help you make your schedule. When building your schedule, you MUST set aside time EVERY week to make prospecting phone calls. Setting aside time to make these calls and sticking to it will help you build a robust schedule. Approximately two-hour time slots three times a week, the same time every week to make as many calls as possible. Remember we just talked about your goal?! JUST SET THE APPOINTMENT TIME, do not try to sell over the phone. Give the customer a few options to meet; this is a huge mistake that salespeople make. When the customer has options, they are more likely to be available.

Your goal making calls and preparation will include:

A.) Have a prepopulated list to call from: Many salespeople waste time during a time block, just trying to find people to call. HAVE A LIST OF CALLS PREPARED!

B.) Passing the gatekeeper: Have ways planned to get around bulldog gatekeepers. They will not all be difficult, but most will. Two ways I used to get around the tough ones were,

    1. AVOID THEM TOTALLY! Call either before they start work or after they go home for the day. Think about who answers the phone when the receptionist is not there, most likely a decision maker!

    2. CALL INTO ANOTHER DEPARTMENT! Accounts payable, the sales department, whatever you choose, in most cases, they will try to get you in touch with the correct person.

C.) JUST handle the decision maker's objection, DON'T SELL OVER THE PHONE! Let's say the decision maker says, "I'm happy with the vendor we use now," you can respond with something like this,

"That's great to hear! My company also gets great compliments like that because of some new business ideas we offer our customers that help them progress in their industry. I would like to see if we can do the same for you and share these ideas in person. I'll be in that area (offer a few times) tomorrow at 1 or Friday at 2, what works best for you?"

This is focusing on THEIR objection and not offering any solutions over the phone. You are simply letting them know you would like to share some ideas with them in person. This will tweak most people's interest and prompt them to maybe take the meeting. This approach will become natural with practice. Come up with ways to handle the most common objections you will hear when making calls.

D.) Know your schedule: An organized salesperson will spend repetitive time in their territory on certain days of the week. Know what areas you will be in Monday through Friday. Try not to just drive around aimlessly all around your territory during the week. Being organized and having a plan will greatly help your mindset and will also help you be able to offer mutable times to meet your customers while prospecting over the phone.

Preparing to meet with your customer.

It is Sunday, and you know that you have done a great job setting up your upcoming week. You have at least eight PLANNED meetings per day set up, you are going to be spending time in certain areas of your territory, and you have some firm goals in place for the week. You have set the stage! What must you do now to enhance EVERY customer experience? It is time to do some RESEARCH! Now I do not recommend doing a tremendous amount of research for every meeting, but I do recommend doing a little. Think about it like this, years ago I did not have the resources that salespeople have today, the internet, LinkedIn, or the company CRM, a lot of the time I was going in blind, which in some cases caused the decision-making process to be longer for the customer. Today, with all these resources at your fingertips, you can gather lots of valuable information to enter a meeting with the upper hand. Look at the website for the company, learn as much as you can to help you position your company with the most benefit to that customer. Next, look up the person you're meeting with on LinkedIn; you can find out if they truly are the decision maker and invite other people to your meeting that you feel will benefit from meeting you. Lastly, a company's CRM will house lots of great information about contacts, previous meetings, and who they meet with. Lots of information can be gathered prior to the meeting. Take advantage of these tools so that your conversation can be progressive and valuable to you and the customer.

ALWAYS carry a notepad – Use this handbook!

A notepad is the sales tool I actually used the most. No matter what laptop, tablet, or electronic device I have open in front of me during sales meetings, a small notepad always comes in handy. I like to make notes when the prospect is talking to me, so they know I am paying attention to them. I would also like to have some notes that I pre-wrote in preparation for the meeting right in front of me, so I would not forget to ask or say certain things. The notes then come in handy when I have got to log all the data into a CRM. The notepad also will come in handy when you must explain something to a customer in writing or must draw a picture to explain a certain situation like we spoke about previously. I cannot tell you how many times I have attended a sales meeting with a rep and they did not have a pad to write on! Drives me NUTS!

Learn all about your company Value Propositions!

EVERY company large and small has some type of value they offer to their customers that they hang their hat on. When it is time for you to get "customer facing," you're going to be expected to be able to articulate that value. Make sure you take the time to learn ALL the value propositions that are offered.

Think about it like this, a doctor's value propositions are all the knowledge, expertise, and medicine they can offer. When you visit the doctor, they will ask many questions to find out what your pains are. Once they come to an educated solution, they will prescribe a remedy. Now, that remedy could be meds, x-ray, or even therapy. They took the necessary time and asked the appropriate questions to arrive at their diagnosis so they could prescribe correctly. You will find a HUGE value in this visit and will recommend this doctor to everyone you know. Let's face it, if you limped into a doctor's office and they prescribed you cold medicine, you would never use that doctor's practice again and tell everyone not to use them. This concept rings true in sales as well. Why do you think a customer decides to NOT do business with you? Plain and simple, you did NOT diagnosis the problem, and you prescribed the incorrect prescription. Let's talk about what is in your Dr. Bag.

What is a Value Proposition you ask? (Although there are many within all the different businesses, I will focus on these four)

Mission Statement

Let's talk about that. First things first, every company normally has a mission statement. A mission statement is a Value Prop! Find out what that is and the values that drive that mission statement. A mission statement will normally be driven by a company's culture. Customers worth having like to do business with people that derive from a progressive culture. Think about that, the decision makers are normally high up in the company and talk about a mission statement with THEIR employees. Now, I am not saying you must recite the mission statement to all your customers, but find a way to weave your culture into your sales process. Decision makers will appreciate that approach and you will differentiate yourself, guaranteed!

Technology

In today's world, it is all about technology. Who has the best App, who has the best website, and the list can go on. The reality is all the different platforms in most cases preform the same tasks. So, do not walk into a customer meeting and think that your APP is going to be the driving force behind their decision to do business with you. The key factor to any customer regarding a technology platform is its ability to solve their business problems. As a professional salesperson, your thought-provoking questions will flush out the business pain that the customer is experiencing, then you will find a way to position that technology to elevate the pain. There is the DIFFERENTI-ATOR! Years ago, I was able to use the "new technology" piece as a huge differentiator. Today, the customer feels if the company does not have apps or new technology, they are behind the times and will decide to do business with another vendor.

Innovation

Take a second and think about what companies you do business with. I can guarantee all of you reading this handbook are the proud owners of a cell phone. I can also guarantee the company that created your phone has a team of people in an office coming up with new innovative ideas to justify and show you a value, so you don't question the amount of the bill and keep paying your bill every month. This concept is important for you to remember when presenting a value prop. Customers need to feel that the business they choose is always on the "cutting edge." Know where your company started and know the path your company is on for future innovation. A great thought-provoking question to ask a customer is "Where do you see your business in 5 years?" When you find out this answer, it will enable you to position your pitch, so the outcome supports the goals of that customer with your upcoming innovation.

Business Expertise

Definition: "A HIGH level of knowledge of the business issues and situations (including the remedies to fix them) that a customer deals with to run their company. Knowledge of the territory you serve is also considered Business Expertise."

The facts are in! Customers value business expertise over building rapport and product knowledge. Do not get me wrong, building rapport and product knowledge are important but at the right time in your sales process. The days of walking into a meeting and talking about the weekend sport stats are dwindling more and more every day. In today's world, customers want to TRUST the people they do business with, and trust comes from asking good questions that reveal customer pains and offering solutions that can immediately help them solve their challenges. Research shows there is a 60% chance a customer will make multiple purchases from the same company. The reason for this is simple, people want to buy from businesses they know they can trust. (Resource - https://blog.zoominfo.com/regain-customer-trust/)

Mindset Preparation

Last but certainly not the least. Salespeople need to be on their game and use their thoughts to get better at sales every day. If you go to bed late, don't take care of yourself, and cause yourself to not feel 100%, it will take a toll on your presentation skills. I learned this early in my career. The last thing you want to do is not feel well and be in a RUSHED mindset prior to an appointment. When you get into the habit of preparing the night before, EVERY DAY, you will get a great night's sleep knowing tomorrow is ALL SET and ready to go. Get your lunch ready, lay out your clothes, try to do anything you can the night before so it's DONE and you can wake up early enough to naturally wake up. If you scramble to get out the door in the morning, your day will automatically start and most likely continue with a rushed mindset for the whole day.

ALWAYS carry your business card

Always remember to carry your business card. There are two main reasons to always have a business card handy. The first reason is the most obvious, you want the customer to remember who you are and be able to refer to it if they forget your name. The second one I learned from lots of trial and error. I urge you to give your business card in the very beginning of the meeting, why? If you do not give your card to the customer in the very beginning, they could use it as an "exit visa" to the meeting. I cannot tell you how many times I was on my game in a meeting, showing lots of value and had the customers head knotting yes to everything, and when the time came to go in for the close, the customer says, "You know what, Joe, let me have your business card, and I'll get back to you" NOOOOO! If I had just taken a quick second to give it to him in the beginning of the meeting, he or she would not have been able to stop me from closing them. Lesson well learned. So, take my advice on this one.

Lastly, make sure your business card is different and unique. Add a QR code! This code should contain a video that is made by you. In the video, you can simply say "It was a pleasure meeting you!" and add a few value propositions that your company offers. This will not only differentiate you but will give the person a reminder of what you look like and provide them with some valuable information about your company! Remember to make this fun! See the example provided below.

Sample business card with QR code – Scan the QR code for content example but remember to make it your own.

Have fun with this, but of course, keep it professional!

Notes you want to remember from this chapter.

_____

_____

_____

_____

_____

_____

_____

_____

_____

_____

_____

_____

_____

_____

_____

_____

_____

_____

_____

_____

_____

_____

_____

_____

_____

CHAPTER FOUR

Field Ready – Meeting with a customer – What is your PPRAAAcess

IT'S MONDAY MORNING, YOU HAVE A ROBUST DAY AHEAD, and you just pulled up for your first meeting. Professionalism starts in the parking lot; you never know who is watching from the office you are about to enter. Funny story, so I pulled up to this office building and parked my car. I was rushing because my mindset was in rush mode. As I'm walking toward the building, I notice a huge glass mirror window. I could not see in, but I had a clear view of my reflection. Since I was in rush mode, I decided to check myself out in the glass mirror window. Checked my beard, made sure nothing was hanging from my nose, and finally proceeded to adjust myself. I then walked into the building where the gatekeeper then took me to the office where I would hold the meeting. On the way to the office, she told me that the team was already in the office anxiously waiting for me to arrive. Well, this office happened to be the one with the glass mirror window. They saw everything. The first words out of the decision makers mouth were, "You're not the first and won't be the last." Everyone in the room busted out laughing. So MAJOR lesson learned. Luckily, everyone was cool about it, and I was able to proceed and have my meeting. I sold that customer that day. I am still trying to figure out if they just felt bad for me. Lol

Time to sit down and have your meeting (utilize the "Meeting PPRAAcess Planner" included with this book for you to download on page 47

Ok, so you are about to sit down and have a meeting, you introduce yourself, hand them your business card, then what do you do? I ask this question a lot in my trainings, and the answers are normally ALL OVER the place. I am shocked to how many salespeople actually really don't know how to start a meeting. Lots of answers revolve around rapport building; I'm always surprised at that because that's what was taught back in the 80s. The concept is not exactly wrong; it just depends on the situation and doing it at the right time.

So, I want to introduce to you my **DIALOG ROAD MAP, your PPRAAAcess.** Your best meetings will happen if you master what happens during your dialog. I would like you to think of this as your **sales PPRAAAcess road map**. Make what you do a repeatable process. Let's dive into each part of the roadmap. **PPRAAA**

1. **Preparation**: We talked about this already. Refer to chapter 3, "Preparing to meet with your customer." Add any notes to your planner prior to the meeting to be ULTRA prepared!

2. **Plug In**: Opening agenda. It is time to sit down and start your meeting. What do you say? Now, I want you to think about that. You have spent a tremendous amount of time and effort to get in front of this person; it is time to differentiate yourself and impress them. If you start your meeting with "How's BIZZ" or "Did you see that game over the weekend?" I can guarantee they will NOT be impressed. In today's world, decision makers want to get down to business, not make friends. Salespeople tend to think that rapport building should happen the minute you sit down. I will respectfully and totally disagree. Yes, rapport building is still important but at the correct time. The customer is looking for you to bring business expertise and solutions to their problems; after you can prove that you can do this, trust will be built. Once trust is built, rapport building becomes genuine, they actually care about you and like you, and that's when relationships will grow. But you must

get to that point first. Let's start with an **Opening Agenda**, a strong opening to a meeting will show professionalism and give the customer a guide on what will be covered in the meeting today.

Here is a sample opening agenda:

Mr. or Mrs. Customer, thank you for taking my meeting today; here is my business card. When we spoke over the phone the other day, I had mentioned that my company has some new business ideas that other companies in your industry have found success with, and I'd like to share them with you today.

I will need to ask a few questions to find out what ideas you will be most interested in. Before I do that though, is there anyone else you would like to include in the meeting that would be interested in what I have to offer, in case the ideas make sense, and you decide to move forward with me today?

(Now if you find out they are the only one that will be attending the meeting today, you can just continue, but if you find out that they would like to involve other people, give them a little time to get them in the meeting, then continue.)

The questions I will begin with will help me understand what business concerns your company might be dealing with and which solution I will introduce to you today, in turn, will help me offer you the solution and the process to implement.

Make sense? . . . GREAT!

Now if all this sound good to you, and you feel we are a good fit, I will be asking for your business today! How does that sound? . . . Great let's get started . . .

Now, a lot of my readers are going to say, "WOW, that sounds very scripted." I would like you to keep in mind that this is just an example. Take the format and make it your own! If you like the verbiage, you are very welcome to use it verbatim, totally up to you! The point I am trying to drive home here is that you must start a meeting with an agenda that takes control of the meeting, gives the customer a road map to what you will be covering, and helps you remove objections that might come up at the end of the meeting. Get creative, and please, just don't start your meeting with "How's Bizz"!

3. **Realize Needs**: Now, as promised in your opening agenda, it's time for you to start asking some good thought-provoking questions. Make sure to have a pad nearby to write the answers down to the questions you ask. A thought-provoking question will get the customer thinking and responding. This is exactly what you want for the customer to be engaged. Your questions **cannot** require a one-word answer, they MUST get that customer thinking. Example of a bad question: "Are you happy with your current vendor?" This question can be answered with a simple "yes" or "no." A better question you could ask would be, *"If you could identify three things you would change about your current vendor what would they be?"* This is poking at their brain, getting them thinking; let them answer the question. This is where your LISTENING skills will be needed. Now, once they answer that question, you write down the answers and "back pocket" them for now, DON'T RESPOND YET, and move on to your next question. These questions are all about realizing the needs or pains the customer is experiencing, even if they do not realize they are experiencing them! You want them to reveal something that you and your company can make better. Remember the doctor example? A doctor will LISTEN before prescribing. This is also why writing the answers down will help you laser focus on an issue. So, make sure your questions revolve around some of the value props you can offer. Again, this could be something that they do not even feel is a problem until you show them that you have new ideas for them that could put their business in a better situation. ASK GREAT QUESTIONS, LISTEN, and write down the answers in your planner.

4. **Advocate**: Now it is time to position a value prop to solve business issues! Once you revile a business pain, you can now choose what value prop to offer to mitigate the challenge. Many salespeople at this point will start rambling off ALL the great things the company offers. Slow down. For now, just choose one or two things to offer and talk about. Also make sure you periodically involve the customer in the conversation. Something like *"Joe, Am I on the right track" "Joe, does this look like it could help you?"* Now, if you are on the

right track, the customer will respond yes, and you might even get a head nod; this is good, because if the customer is nodding their head in agreeance and understanding throughout, your presentation it is extremely hard for them to say no to your offering at the end of the meeting. If things are going well and you have the customers head nodding yes, let's advance the sale.

5. Advance: Salespeople are sometimes afraid to ask for the business. Just keep this in mind; if you followed your process, starting with an agenda, asking great questions, revealing pains, positioning a value prop to solve the issue, and gaining agreeance to your solution, IT'S TIME TO ASK FOR THE BUSINESS!! Let's talk about how that might sound. *"Mr. Customer, now that I have showed you a solution to your business issue, is there anything stopping you from doing business with me today?* **Immanently after this statement, be silent**. Let the customer process that question and answer you. In most cases, if you follow a process and execute in the way we talked about, a positive outcome will follow. Years ago, we referred to it as "the first person to talk loses." Some of you will remember that concept.

6. ACT: Now, whether you wrote a deal or not, you have to put some action plans in place for some next steps with that customer on your schedule. An important part of your schedule every week is having follow up activities with your past meetings. This will guarantee that you have a robust schedule full of productive customer interactions in the future.

Ladies and gentlemen, that's how to have an effective meeting! Think back to all your past experiences, and I can guarantee that you have already executed some of these concepts in your previous meetings. You just needed someone to put it all together and give it some structure. Well, here you go. Take the time to master this PPRAAAcess, Practice with your co-workers, your spouse, your friends, and do it EVERY TIME with a customer during a meeting. With practice, you will find yourself automatically executing every step, every time, and success will follow!

This handbook/workbook contains a PPRAAAcess planner guide template on page 47. Review this planner. Everything we have talked about in this chapter is laid out for you as a reminder and a guide to use during a meeting. When I created this handbook/workbook, my goal was that whoever had it in their position could use it to plan their weeks as well as have a tool to use during a meeting. I hope this helps.

Notes you want to remember from this chapter.

_____

_____

_____

_____

_____

_____

_____

_____

_____

_____

_____

_____

_____

_____

_____

_____

_____

_____

_____

_____

_____

_____

_____

_____

_____

CHAPTER FIVE

Follow up Whether You Made a Sale or Not

OK, THIS IS WHERE SALESPEOPLE DEFINE THEMSELVES as being the best at what they do, or just another mediocre salesperson struggling to make a living. It ALL revolves around communication. After EVERY customer interaction, there must be next steps with that person. A lot of salespeople think that after they make a sale, their job is done. I am here to tell you that is not the case. To convey this particularly important piece of the process, I have compiled some next step examples below.

You sold the customer!

1. Set up a communication schedule with that person.

2. A thank you email, video, or handwritten card.

3. On your future schedule, reserve time to meet back with that person regularly. There were probably some other products or services that you did not get a chance to talk about in your first meeting. (The industry you work in will help you figure out how often to meet with that person.)

4. Set up meetings with other people within that company. (Accounts payable, purchasing manager, maybe even a salesperson from that company) Network with as many people as you can, you never know who they know and what you can do for each other.

5. Set up a lunch where you can explain more about your company to a larger group of people while they enjoy some food. (HUGE DIFFERENTIATOR!!)

6. In preparation of the first delivery to your new customer, make sure you communicate to EVERYONE involved that this is a new customer delivery and you want to make sure all goes as promised.

7. Depending on the product or service you sell, try to be at the location of delivery for that customer's first few orders.

8. Also, if you can't be physically there, make sure you are available and ready to take a call in case any issues arise with the first order delivered.

9. Make a courtesy call as soon as you can to connect with your customer to ensure that they were satisfied and happy with the product. A lot of sales-people fight me on this one because they feel it will open a can of worms . . . I say LET IT! If your customer is NOT 100% satisfied, you need to know and FIX IT. If you are not aware of a dissatisfied customer, they will move on to another vendor, and if your communication is poor with them, you will never know. This is why lots of salespeople say, "I haven't heard from so and so in a long time, and no orders have been placed. I wonder what happened." Let me fill you in, they were unhappy, and no one followed up after they placed a first order. DON'T BE THAT SALESPERSON!

10. Ask for referrals—happy customers will refer you to other customers. When a recommendation comes from someone who has actually used your services, it has an extra layer of credibility and trust. Existing customers make the best advocates because third-party claims of problem solving carry more weight than self-promotion. I have found that customers are willing to refer because they know how important referrals are, and if you have built trust and shown business expertise, people will want to help you succeed.

11. Holiday Awareness: I always kept a list of my special customers. Remember, not every customer will make the holiday list, but for the ones that do, I would always visit around the holidays and you can guarantee that my hands would be full of holiday cheer. A handwritten card with a gift to the office, thanking them for their business. I promise, this goes a LONG way.

I am sure there are hundred other things that you can think about now that I got your juices flowing with this short list. Just focus on the right direction of staying in touch with your customers and good, reliable, long-term business relationships will follow.

Now, you did not sell the customer.

Do not beat yourself up. You are not going to sell every single customer. But let us keep in mind that we can learn from these losses. We want to ask questions like *"Can you help me understand what your key decision factors were?"* and *"Was there anything we could have done better or differently in this situation to improve our chances of winning the deal?"* It tells the customer that we are sincere and interested in helping ourself improve. By knowing the answers to these questions, you will help yourself understand and improve on your process better with future customer meetings. The final piece that I think is critically important is to continue to treat that prospect as if it is a customer.

Follow up is still the key:

1. Still send a thank you email, video, or handwritten card. Believe it or not, I have had customers call me after they said no and change their mind because I took the time to still say thank you for taking the time to meet me. You never know.

2. Keep them on your email or mail chain. You never know if a situation in their future will cause them to remember you and give you a call.

3. Let's ask for a future meeting, obviously not next week, but in the future. If a customer declines doing business with you NOW, they might feel obligated to review your products and services again in the future. Ask for a simple scheduled "check in meeting." Let's face it, it is better than walking out with nada! You have nothing to lose by asking, so ask!

4. Invite them to a webinar or send them a value-added article. Now that you have met them and know some of their pains, you might come across something that might peak their interest. Send it to them!

Some of you reading this might be saying "Wow, Joe is telling me to stalk my lost deals." By no means am I telling you this. Often, we are just frustrated and disappointed that we didn't close a deal, and we just move on to the next customer. We forget that there are incredible lessons that we can learn by following up and communicating with that customer and seeing what we can take away from that opportunity that didn't work out. And maybe, just maybe, watering the seed we planted for future business with that customer. Like I said previously, if you do absolutely nothing with that lost opportunity, most likely nothing will follow.

Notes you want to remember from this chapter.

_____

_____

_____

_____

_____

_____

_____

_____

_____

_____

_____

_____

_____

_____

_____

_____

_____

_____

_____

_____

_____

_____

_____

_____

_____

CHAPTER SIX

Business Networking (GROW YOUR CONNECTION PIPELINE)

I **TELL THIS STORY ALMOST IN EVERY ONE OF MY TRAININGS.** Years ago, when my sons were young, they would play lots of sports. Every weekend and sometimes during the week I would find myself on a field watching my boys play sports. Now, as you can imagine, I obviously was not the only parent on the sidelines. Now, being in sales my whole life, I would try to find opportunity EVERYWHERE I went, striking up a conversation, handing out a business brochure with my business card, and networking as much as I could. As the years went on, I would find myself sitting alone on the field. Yes, a new parent would show up occasionally, but I almost feel they were warned about me. LOL. To be honest, I did not care; this was me, this is what I did to make money for my family, this is what I was good at, and tried to capitalize on every interaction. Some new customers came from my efforts on those fields, so to me, I felt JOB WELL DONE.

Every day in sales is a new day. You have chosen to be in this profession. Today might be the day you meet and connect with a person that will give you the BIG DEAL. You must be hungry and thinking this way all the time.

If you are not networking and building a huge connection pipeline, you are not going to be as successful as you can be.

That is why I feel this section is so valuable. **Who you know**, is equally **AS IMPORTIANT** as **what you know**. Throughout this reading, I have stressed to you that business expertise is one of the most important attributes of a salesperson. Well in this section, I will talk about growing your pipeline of people that actually find this attribute important.

I will agree that most huge networking events can be tough. I have found many of them to be full of would-be entrepreneurs and pushy salespeople only looking out for themselves. My suggestion is to find or even create groups of smart people with shared values getting together to see how they can help each other. This will move you forward in your career.

Start off with other salespeople in your office. When I first started out, I would meet with the salespeople I worked with outside the once-a-week office sales meetings. I would set up a time for coffee or lunch and lots of brain storming. I compared success and failures; this alone I found to be so valuable. I would learn some dos and don'ts while collaborating with my own team. This type of networking surrounds you with like-minded people, feeding off each other's excitement. Especially if you are just getting started in your career or a seasoned rep going through a difficult time, meeting people who have been there, failed, or succeeded, is a great way to boost your morale.

I then moved on to competitor friendships. I was in a business that I would frequently bump into other salespeople from the competitors. Instead of dirty looks and talking behind each other's backs, I would grow a professional relationship. Have a cup of coffee, maybe a quick lunch. I am a firm believer in knowing the "demands" that I am up against every day. Now, make sure you keep your professionalism in check; do not give any trade secrets, but definitely be open to collaborating. Often times, my phone would ring, and it would be one of those competitor salespeople saying, "Go get this one, I had no luck with them." And low and behold, we were helping each other rather than banging heads in the field. When you give your experience and **selected** knowledge freely, others will follow suite. So, not only does this type of networking help you understand the surroundings better, but it gives you the opportunity to learn from others who might be masters in your industry. This is a concept that I have seen proven to work.

What are your own motivations to networking?

Remember, bringing value to other people in networking events is vital to future event success and attendance. You do not want to be that person that just keeps asking for information and not adding anything to the conversation. Ask yourself and prepare to provide other people with valuable insight that you have gained from the field. Share some industry experience, providing them with genuine advice on how you were able to provide a solution to a particular customer that resulted in a sale. Good books to read, like this one. Try to be the best influence you can be at these events. You will find more invites in the future to attend more.

Let's talk about etiquette at these networking events.

Start off with making sure you are being genuine, and praise other people's accomplishments. We ALL as salespeople have the problem of thinking what to say next when someone else is talking. I do it all the time. What we must remember is that people can read this disinterest, and it will cause them to avoid you (same rings true when you're in front of a customer), remember that. Now is the time for ears up! Be genuinely listening to them and complement them if needed. This is the key to create a genuine connection. Success at these events is based on your appreciation of a value someone shares with you along with you wanting to help other people. Your success and personal takeaways will come if you practice proper etiquette. Also, some of these events do not allow you to hand out your business card, this is crazy to me, but most will allow for business card sharing. Be sure to hand out your awesome new QR-coded business card! HUGE differentiator!

Lastly, follow-ups after the events are just as important as follow-ups after customer meetings.

Do not let all the time and effort go to waste. Similar to a follow-up after a customer meeting, we must stay in touch with the valuable connections after a networking event. Time is of the essence. A few tips to follow.

1. **Send a thank you email, video, or handwritten card** within 24 hours of the event. The sooner you do it, the better. Everyone met lots of people; if you find a value to stay connected with someone in particular, strike while the iron is hot!

2. **Connect on LinkedIn**. This will only make the connection stronger. Many people share what they see as valuable information on LinkedIn. The more connections they have, the more people they get the message to. The more followers, the merrier!

3. **Maybe it's time to ask for a personal professional meeting**. Depending on how well the networking event went, meeting someone particular, and how deep your conversation went with them, it's time to decide if you want to extend a coffee meeting to share some more ideas. Maybe word it like, *"I'd like to get a chance to continue our conversation we were having at the event."*

Remember, these networking events can go either way; you might find a huge value in one, or the next might be a total waste of time. Going to these with this mindset is my advice. Networking has huge advantages to salespeople. Find your niche events and grow as much as you can with them over the years. The payoff will speak for itself.

Notes you want to remember from this chapter.

CHAPTER SEVEN

A Successful Attitude

A GREAT ATTITUDE IS THE "BIG SECRETE" TO SUCCESS in any sales position. People will mirror a great attitude. People meaning, customers, co-workers, managers, pretty much anyone you come in contact with will sense a person who has a great attitude. Think about this, would you rather be around people sharing a positive mood or people who are showing negativity? The answer is clear. Now, how do we get and maintain this status? Well, as I said earlier in this reading, mindset of a salesperson will blaze the trail to success! So, it all starts with you!

Take a second and think about it like this.

Growth in sales and your personal life is where it all begins. When you take the time to perfect your craft by learning, reading, taking good advice, and putting it to work for you, success becomes easier to attain. The more success you have, the more you become valuable to your company. You have perfected your craft and can execute a sales process flawlessly. A respect level for you as an employee skyrockets, and you become known for your achievements. You own the room when you walk into a sales meeting. People start asking you for advice and want to bounce ideas off you. Hell, they want to be you. You show professionalism and your attitude attracts others. With all of this going for you, it is inevitable that your paycheck reflects all your hard work constantly exuding success and your infectious attitude. Your family life is abundant, and your spouse and family are proud of your success. Your family wants for nothing, you vacation in all the exotic islands, and your garage has your childhood favorite vehicles, and the best part of all of this is that you do not consider what you do a job anymore. You cannot wait to wake up every day and make more money. You love your life . . . All sounds good? Well, it all can be a reality! It just depends on YOU.

All Your Outcomes depend on you.

You are not sitting in a cubicle. You are not a person that hopes for a 2% raise every December; your life and the way you live is not captive to a mediocre salary. You are the person that wakes up every day and has unlimited potential to drive your happiness and income in any direction you choose. That is the full glory of a sales career. Wake up every day and jump out of bed. Today could be the big one! If your mindset is not programed this way, a sales career may not be the best choice for you. As I mentioned hunger is your friend. Be hungry to learn EVERYDAY about what you do and how to advance your life. Never think you know everything in sales. Sales changes every day, people change every day, in turn, your sales mindset must be fluid and willing to conform and change every day. Help others learn, become the mentor, and spread your knowledge; you will only become a better for it. If you ever doubted this next statement, I am here to confirm, salespeople are a part of the most important people in the world. The companies that drive our economy and our way of life depend on salespeople succeeding every minute of every day. Stay away from negative people; they will only try to bring you down with them. Take one thing at a time from this reading, choose a concept and prefect it, and then move on to the next. If you try to change everything you do all at once, I guarantee frustration will kick in and you will question if this career choice was the best for you. One thing at a time.

Good Luck!

Notes you want to remember from this chapter.

_____

_____

_____

_____

_____

_____

_____

_____

_____

_____

_____

_____

_____

_____

_____

_____

_____

_____

_____

_____

_____

_____

_____

_____

_____

_____

_____

_____

_____

_____

MEETING PPRAAACESS PLANNER

The information on this planner has been compiled from the information you learned in this book. This planner will help guide you through the meeting process while with a customer. Actively use this planner every day! In time, the process will become second nature.

The QR code below will bring you to where you can download the planner!

SCAN ME

DAY PLANNER

Every Day	Monday	Tuesday	Wednesday
	Date: /	Date: /	Date: /
6:30am			
7:00am			
7:30am			
8:00am			
8:30am			
9:00am			
9:30am			
10:00am			
10:30am			
11:00am			
11:30am			
12:00pm			
12:30pm			
1:00pm			
1:30pm			
2:00pm			
2:30pm			
3:00pm			
3:30pm			
4:00pm			
4:30pm			
5:00pm			
5:30pm			
6:00pm			
7:00pm			

Goals For Today ----

Every Day	Thursday	Friday	Saturday
	Date: /	Date: /	Date: /
6:30am --------			
7:00am --------			
7:30am --------			
8:00am --------			
8:30am --------			
9:00am --------			
9:30am --------			
10:00am --------			
10:30am --------			
11:00am --------			
11:30am --------			
12:00pm --------			
12:30pm --------			
1:00pm --------			
1:30pm --------			
2:00pm --------			
2:30pm --------			
3:00pm --------			
3:30pm --------			
4:00pm --------			
4:30pm --------			
5:00pm --------			
5:30pm --------			
6:00pm --------			
7:00pm --------			

Goals For Today ----

Every Day	Monday	Tuesday	Wednesday
	Date: /	Date: /	Date: /
6:30am			
7:00am			
7:30am			
8:00am			
8:30am			
9:00am			
9:30am			
10:00am			
10:30am			
11:00am			
11:30am			
12:00pm			
12:30pm			
1:00pm			
1:30pm			
2:00pm			
2:30pm			
3:00pm			
3:30pm			
4:00pm			
4:30pm			
5:00pm			
5:30pm			
6:00pm			
7:00pm			

Goals For Today ----

	Date: /	Date: /	Date: /
Every Day	Thursday	Friday	Saturday
6:30am			
7:00am			
7:30am			
8:00am			
8:30am			
9:00am			
9:30am			
10:00am			
10:30am			
11:00am			
11:30am			
12:00pm			
12:30pm			
1:00pm			
1:30pm			
2:00pm			
2:30pm			
3:00pm			
3:30pm			
4:00pm			
4:30pm			
5:00pm			
5:30pm			
6:00pm			
7:00pm			

Goals For Today ----

| | Date: / | Date: / | Date: / |
Every Day	Monday	Tuesday	Wednesday
6:30am -------			
7:00am -------			
7:30am -------			
8:00am -------			
8:30am -------			
9:00am -------			
9:30am -------			
10:00am -------			
10:30am -------			
11:00am -------			
11:30am -------			
12:00pm -------			
12:30pm -------			
1:00pm -------			
1:30pm -------			
2:00pm -------			
2:30pm -------			
3:00pm -------			
3:30pm -------			
4:00pm -------			
4:30pm -------			
5:00pm -------			
5:30pm -------			
6:00pm -------			
7:00pm -------			

Goals For Today ----

Every Day	Thursday	Friday	Saturday
	Date: /	Date: /	Date: /
6:30am ----------			
7:00am ----------			
7:30am ----------			
8:00am ----------			
8:30am ----------			
9:00am ----------			
9:30am ----------			
10:00am ----------			
10:30am ----------			
11:00am ----------			
11:30am ----------			
12:00pm ----------			
12:30pm ----------			
1:00pm ----------			
1:30pm ----------			
2:00pm ----------			
2:30pm ----------			
3:00pm ----------			
3:30pm ----------			
4:00pm ----------			
4:30pm ----------			
5:00pm ----------			
5:30pm ----------			
6:00pm ----------			
7:00pm ----------			

Goals For Today ----

	Date: /	Date: /	Date: /
Every Day	**Monday**	**Tuesday**	**Wednesday**
6:30am -------			
7:00am -------			
7:30am			
8:00am -------			
8:30am			
9:00am -------			
9:30am			
10:00am -------			
10:30am			
11:00am -------			
11:30am			
12:00pm -------			
12:30pm			
1:00pm -------			
1:30pm			
2:00pm -------			
2:30pm			
3:00pm -------			
3:30pm			
4:00pm -------			
4:30pm			
5:00pm -------			
5:30pm			
6:00pm -------			
7:00pm -------			

Goals For Today ----

Every Day	Thursday	Friday	Saturday
	Date: /	Date: /	Date: /
6:30am --------			
7:00am --------			
7:30am --------			
8:00am --------			
8:30am --------			
9:00am --------			
9:30am --------			
10:00am -------			
10:30am -------			
11:00am -------			
11:30am -------			
12:00pm			
12:30pm			
1:00pm --------			
1:30pm --------			
2:00pm --------			
2:30pm			
3:00pm --------			
3:30pm --------			
4:00pm --------			
4:30pm			
5:00pm --------			
5:30pm --------			
6:00pm --------			
7:00pm --------			

Goals For Today ----

Every Day	Monday	Tuesday	Wednesday
	Date: /	Date: /	Date: /
6:30am			
7:00am			
7:30am			
8:00am			
8:30am			
9:00am			
9:30am			
10:00am			
10:30am			
11:00am			
11:30am			
12:00pm			
12:30pm			
1:00pm			
1:30pm			
2:00pm			
2:30pm			
3:00pm			
3:30pm			
4:00pm			
4:30pm			
5:00pm			
5:30pm			
6:00pm			
7:00pm			

Goals For Today ----

Every Day	Thursday	Friday	Saturday
	Date: / /	Date: / /	Date: / /
6:30am			
7:00am			
7:30am			
8:00am			
8:30am			
9:00am			
9:30am			
10:00am			
10:30am			
11:00am			
11:30am			
12:00pm			
12:30pm			
1:00pm			
1:30pm			
2:00pm			
2:30pm			
3:00pm			
3:30pm			
4:00pm			
4:30pm			
5:00pm			
5:30pm			
6:00pm			
7:00pm			

Goals For Today ----

Every Day	Date: / Monday	Date: / Tuesday	Date: / Wednesday
6:30am			
7:00am			
7:30am			
8:00am			
8:30am			
9:00am			
9:30am			
10:00am			
10:30am			
11:00am			
11:30am			
12:00pm			
12:30pm			
1:00pm			
1:30pm			
2:00pm			
2:30pm			
3:00pm			
3:30pm			
4:00pm			
4:30pm			
5:00pm			
5:30pm			
6:00pm			
7:00pm			

Goals For Today ----

Every Day	Thursday	Friday	Saturday
	Date: /	Date: /	Date: /
6:30am			
7:00am			
7:30am			
8:00am			
8:30am			
9:00am			
9:30am			
10:00am			
10:30am			
11:00am			
11:30am			
12:00pm			
12:30pm			
1:00pm			
1:30pm			
2:00pm			
2:30pm			
3:00pm			
3:30pm			
4:00pm			
4:30pm			
5:00pm			
5:30pm			
6:00pm			
7:00pm			

Goals For Today -----

Every Day	Date: / Monday	Date: / Tuesday	Date: / Wednesday
6:30am			
7:00am			
7:30am			
8:00am			
8:30am			
9:00am			
9:30am			
10:00am			
10:30am			
11:00am			
11:30am			
12:00pm			
12:30pm			
1:00pm			
1:30pm			
2:00pm			
2:30pm			
3:00pm			
3:30pm			
4:00pm			
4:30pm			
5:00pm			
5:30pm			
6:00pm			
7:00pm			

Goals For Today ----

Every Day	Thursday	Friday	Saturday
	Date: /	Date: /	Date: /
6:30am			
7:00am			
7:30am			
8:00am			
8:30am			
9:00am			
9:30am			
10:00am			
10:30am			
11:00am			
11:30am			
12:00pm			
12:30pm			
1:00pm			
1:30pm			
2:00pm			
2:30pm			
3:00pm			
3:30pm			
4:00pm			
4:30pm			
5:00pm			
5:30pm			
6:00pm			
7:00pm			

Goals For Today ----

	Date: /	Date: /	Date: /
Every Day	**Monday**	**Tuesday**	**Wednesday**
6:30am			
7:00am			
7:30am			
8:00am			
8:30am			
9:00am			
9:30am			
10:00am			
10:30am			
11:00am			
11:30am			
12:00pm			
12:30pm			
1:00pm			
1:30pm			
2:00pm			
2:30pm			
3:00pm			
3:30pm			
4:00pm			
4:30pm			
5:00pm			
5:30pm			
6:00pm			
7:00pm			

Goals For Today ----

Date: /   Date: /   Date: /

Every Day	Thursday	Friday	Saturday
6:30am --------			
7:00am --------			
7:30am --------			
8:00am --------			
8:30am --------			
9:00am --------			
9:30am --------			
10:00am --------			
10:30am --------			
11:00am --------			
11:30am --------			
12:00pm --------			
12:30pm --------			
1:00pm --------			
1:30pm --------			
2:00pm --------			
2:30pm --------			
3:00pm --------			
3:30pm --------			
4:00pm --------			
4:30pm --------			
5:00pm --------			
5:30pm --------			
6:00pm --------			
7:00pm --------			

Goals For Today ----

Every Day	Date: / Monday	Date: / Tuesday	Date: / Wednesday
6:30am			
7:00am			
7:30am			
8:00am			
8:30am			
9:00am			
9:30am			
10:00am			
10:30am			
11:00am			
11:30am			
12:00pm			
12:30pm			
1:00pm			
1:30pm			
2:00pm			
2:30pm			
3:00pm			
3:30pm			
4:00pm			
4:30pm			
5:00pm			
5:30pm			
6:00pm			
7:00pm			

Goals For Today ----

Every Day	Thursday	Friday	Saturday
	Date: /	Date: /	Date: /
6:30am			
7:00am			
7:30am			
8:00am			
8:30am			
9:00am			
9:30am			
10:00am			
10:30am			
11:00am			
11:30am			
12:00pm			
12:30pm			
1:00pm			
1:30pm			
2:00pm			
2:30pm			
3:00pm			
3:30pm			
4:00pm			
4:30pm			
5:00pm			
5:30pm			
6:00pm			
7:00pm			

Goals For Today ----

	Date: /	Date: /	Date: /
Every Day	**Monday**	**Tuesday**	**Wednesday**
6:30am--------			
7:00am--------			
7:30am			
8:00am--------			
8:30am			
9:00am--------			
9:30am			
10:00am-------			
10:30am			
11:00am-------			
11:30am			
12:00pm-------			
12:30pm			
1:00pm --------			
1:30pm			
2:00pm--------			
2:30pm			
3:00pm--------			
3:30pm			
4:00pm--------			
4:30pm			
5:00pm--------			
5:30pm			
6:00pm--------			
7:00pm--------			

Goals For Today -----

Every Day	Thursday	Friday	Saturday
	Date: /	Date: /	Date: /
6:30am --------			
7:00am--------			
7:30am			
8:00am--------			
8:30am			
9:00am--------			
9:30am			
10:00am--------			
10:30am			
11:00am--------			
11:30am			
12:00pm			
12:30pm			
1:00pm --------			
1:30pm			
2:00pm--------			
2:30pm			
3:00pm--------			
3:30pm			
4:00pm--------			
4:30pm			
5:00pm--------			
5:30pm			
6:00pm--------			
7:00pm--------			

Goals For Today ----

	Date: /	Date: /	Date: /
Every Day	**Monday**	**Tuesday**	**Wednesday**
6:30am -------			
7:00am-------			
7:30am-------			
8:00am-------			
8:30am-------			
9:00am-------			
9:30am-------			
10:00am-------			
10:30am-------			
11:00am-------			
11:30am-------			
12:00pm-------			
12:30pm-------			
1:00pm-------			
1:30pm-------			
2:00pm-------			
2:30pm-------			
3:00pm-------			
3:30pm-------			
4:00pm-------			
4:30pm-------			
5:00pm-------			
5:30pm-------			
6:00pm-------			
7:00pm-------			

Goals For Today ----

Every Day	Thursday	Friday	Saturday
	Date: /	Date: /	Date: /
6:30am --------			
7:00am --------			
7:30am --------			
8:00am --------			
8:30am --------			
9:00am --------			
9:30am --------			
10:00am -------			
10:30am -------			
11:00am -------			
11:30am -------			
12:00pm -------			
12:30pm -------			
1:00pm --------			
1:30pm --------			
2:00pm --------			
2:30pm --------			
3:00pm --------			
3:30pm --------			
4:00pm --------			
4:30pm --------			
5:00pm --------			
5:30pm --------			
6:00pm --------			
7:00pm --------			

Goals For Today ------

| | Date: / | Date: / | Date: / |
Every Day	Monday	Tuesday	Wednesday
6:30am --------			
7:00am --------			
7:30am			
8:00am --------			
8:30am			
9:00am--------			
9:30am			
10:00am--------			
10:30am			
11:00am--------			
11:30am			
12:00pm			
12:30pm			
1:00pm --------			
1:30pm			
2:00pm--------			
2:30pm			
3:00pm--------			
3:30pm --------			
4:00pm			
4:30pm			
5:00pm--------			
5:30pm			
6:00pm--------			
7:00pm--------			

Goals For Today ----

Every Day	Thursday	Friday	Saturday
	Date: /	Date: /	Date: /
6:30am			
7:00am			
7:30am			
8:00am			
8:30am			
9:00am			
9:30am			
10:00am			
10:30am			
11:00am			
11:30am			
12:00pm			
12:30pm			
1:00pm			
1:30pm			
2:00pm			
2:30pm			
3:00pm			
3:30pm			
4:00pm			
4:30pm			
5:00pm			
5:30pm			
6:00pm			
7:00pm			

Goals For Today ----

Every Day	Monday Date: /	Tuesday Date: /	Wednesday Date: /
6:30am			
7:00am			
7:30am			
8:00am			
8:30am			
9:00am			
9:30am			
10:00am			
10:30am			
11:00am			
11:30am			
12:00pm			
12:30pm			
1:00pm			
1:30pm			
2:00pm			
2:30pm			
3:00pm			
3:30pm			
4:00pm			
4:30pm			
5:00pm			
5:30pm			
6:00pm			
7:00pm			

Goals For Today ----

| | Date: / | Date: / | Date: / |
Every Day	Thursday	Friday	Saturday
6:30am			
7:00am			
7:30am			
8:00am			
8:30am			
9:00am			
9:30am			
10:00am			
10:30am			
11:00am			
11:30am			
12:00pm			
12:30pm			
1:00pm			
1:30pm			
2:00pm			
2:30pm			
3:00pm			
3:30pm			
4:00pm			
4:30pm			
5:00pm			
5:30pm			
6:00pm			
7:00pm			
Goals For Today ----			

	Date: /	Date: /	Date: /
Every Day	**Monday**	**Tuesday**	**Wednesday**
6:30am			
7:00am			
7:30am			
8:00am			
8:30am			
9:00am			
9:30am			
10:00am			
10:30am			
11:00am			
11:30am			
12:00pm			
12:30pm			
1:00pm			
1:30pm			
2:00pm			
2:30pm			
3:00pm			
3:30pm			
4:00pm			
4:30pm			
5:00pm			
5:30pm			
6:00pm			
7:00pm			

Goals For Today ----

Every Day	Thursday	Friday	Saturday
	Date: /	Date: /	Date: /
6:30am -------			
7:00am -------			
7:30am -------			
8:00am -------			
8:30am -------			
9:00am -------			
9:30am -------			
10:00am ------			
10:30am ------			
11:00am ------			
11:30am ------			
12:00pm ------			
12:30pm ------			
1:00pm -------			
1:30pm -------			
2:00pm -------			
2:30pm -------			
3:00pm -------			
3:30pm -------			
4:00pm -------			
4:30pm -------			
5:00pm -------			
5:30pm -------			
6:00pm -------			
7:00pm -------			

Goals For Today -----

| | Date: / | Date: / | Date: / |
Every Day	Monday	Tuesday	Wednesday
6:30am --------			
7:00am --------			
7:30am			
8:00am			
8:30am			
9:00am --------			
9:30am			
10:00am --------			
10:30am			
11:00am --------			
11:30am			
12:00pm --------			
12:30pm			
1:00pm --------			
1:30pm			
2:00pm			
2:30pm			
3:00pm --------			
3:30pm			
4:00pm --------			
4:30pm			
5:00pm --------			
5:30pm			
6:00pm --------			
7:00pm --------			

Goals For Today ----

Every Day	Thursday	Friday	Saturday
	Date: /	Date: /	Date: /
6:30am			
7:00am			
7:30am			
8:00am			
8:30am			
9:00am			
9:30am			
10:00am			
10:30am			
11:00am			
11:30am			
12:00pm			
12:30pm			
1:00pm			
1:30pm			
2:00pm			
2:30pm			
3:00pm			
3:30pm			
4:00pm			
4:30pm			
5:00pm			
5:30pm			
6:00pm			
7:00pm			

Goals For Today ----

Every Day	Monday	Tuesday	Wednesday
	Date: /	Date: /	Date: /
6:30am			
7:00am			
7:30am			
8:00am			
8:30am			
9:00am			
9:30am			
10:00am			
10:30am			
11:00am			
11:30am			
12:00pm			
12:30pm			
1:00pm			
1:30pm			
2:00pm			
2:30pm			
3:00pm			
3:30pm			
4:00pm			
4:30pm			
5:00pm			
5:30pm			
6:00pm			
7:00pm			

Goals For Today ----

Every Day	Thursday	Friday	Saturday
	Date: /	Date: /	Date: /
6:30am			
7:00am			
7:30am			
8:00am			
8:30am			
9:00am			
9:30am			
10:00am			
10:30am			
11:00am			
11:30am			
12:00pm			
12:30pm			
1:00pm			
1:30pm			
2:00pm			
2:30pm			
3:00pm			
3:30pm			
4:00pm			
4:30pm			
5:00pm			
5:30pm			
6:00pm			
7:00pm			

Goals For Today ----

Every Day	Date: / Monday	Date: / Tuesday	Date: / Wednesday
6:30am			
7:00am			
7:30am			
8:00am			
8:30am			
9:00am			
9:30am			
10:00am			
10:30am			
11:00am			
11:30am			
12:00pm			
12:30pm			
1:00pm			
1:30pm			
2:00pm			
2:30pm			
3:00pm			
3:30pm			
4:00pm			
4:30pm			
5:00pm			
5:30pm			
6:00pm			
7:00pm			

Goals For Today ----

Every Day	Thursday	Friday	Saturday
	Date: /	Date: /	Date: /
6:30am			
7:00am			
7:30am			
8:00am			
8:30am			
9:00am			
9:30am			
10:00am			
10:30am			
11:00am			
11:30am			
12:00pm			
12:30pm			
1:00pm			
1:30pm			
2:00pm			
2:30pm			
3:00pm			
3:30pm			
4:00pm			
4:30pm			
5:00pm			
5:30pm			
6:00pm			
7:00pm			

Goals For Today ----

| | Date: / | Date: / | Date: / |
Every Day	Monday	Tuesday	Wednesday
6:30am --------			
7:00am --------			
7:30am --------			
8:00am --------			
8:30am --------			
9:00am --------			
9:30am --------			
10:00am -------			
10:30am -------			
11:00am -------			
11:30am -------			
12:00pm -------			
12:30pm -------			
1:00pm --------			
1:30pm --------			
2:00pm --------			
2:30pm --------			
3:00pm --------			
3:30pm --------			
4:00pm --------			
4:30pm --------			
5:00pm --------			
5:30pm --------			
6:00pm --------			
7:00pm --------			

Goals For Today ----

Every Day	Thursday	Friday	Saturday
	Date: /	Date: /	Date: /
6:30am ────────			
7:00am ────────			
7:30am ────────			
8:00am ────────			
8:30am ────────			
9:00am ────────			
9:30am ────────			
10:00am ────────			
10:30am ────────			
11:00am ────────			
11:30am ────────			
12:00pm ────────			
12:30pm ────────			
1:00pm ────────			
1:30pm ────────			
2:00pm ────────			
2:30pm ────────			
3:00pm ────────			
3:30pm ────────			
4:00pm ────────			
4:30pm ────────			
5:00pm ────────			
5:30pm ────────			
6:00pm ────────			
7:00pm ────────			

Goals For Today ──────

Every Day	Monday	Tuesday	Wednesday
	Date: /	Date: /	Date: /
6:30am			
7:00am			
7:30am			
8:00am			
8:30am			
9:00am			
9:30am			
10:00am			
10:30am			
11:00am			
11:30am			
12:00pm			
12:30pm			
1:00pm			
1:30pm			
2:00pm			
2:30pm			
3:00pm			
3:30pm			
4:00pm			
4:30pm			
5:00pm			
5:30pm			
6:00pm			
7:00pm			

Goals For Today ----

| | Date: / | Date: / | Date: / |
Every Day	Thursday	Friday	Saturday
6:30am ----------			
7:00am ----------			
7:30am ----------			
8:00am ----------			
8:30am ----------			
9:00am ----------			
9:30am ----------			
10:00am ----------			
10:30am ----------			
11:00am ----------			
11:30am ----------			
12:00pm ----------			
12:30pm ----------			
1:00pm ----------			
1:30pm ----------			
2:00pm ----------			
2:30pm ----------			
3:00pm ----------			
3:30pm ----------			
4:00pm ----------			
4:30pm ----------			
5:00pm ----------			
5:30pm ----------			
6:00pm ----------			
7:00pm ----------			

Goals For Today ----

Every Day	Monday	Tuesday	Wednesday
6:30am --------			
7:00am --------			
7:30am --------			
8:00am --------			
8:30am --------			
9:00am --------			
9:30am --------			
10:00am --------			
10:30am --------			
11:00am --------			
11:30am --------			
12:00pm --------			
12:30pm --------			
1:00pm --------			
1:30pm --------			
2:00pm --------			
2:30pm --------			
3:00pm --------			
3:30pm --------			
4:00pm --------			
4:30pm --------			
5:00pm --------			
5:30pm --------			
6:00pm --------			
7:00pm --------			

Goals For Today -----

| Date: / | Date: / | Date: / |

Every Day	Thursday	Friday	Saturday
6:30am --------			
7:00am --------			
7:30am --------			
8:00am --------			
8:30am			
9:00am --------			
9:30am			
10:00am			
10:30am			
11:00am --------			
11:30am			
12:00pm --------			
12:30pm			
1:00pm --------			
1:30pm			
2:00pm			
2:30pm			
3:00pm --------			
3:30pm			
4:00pm --------			
4:30pm			
5:00pm --------			
5:30pm			
6:00pm --------			
7:00pm --------			

Goals For Today ----

	Date: /	Date: /	Date: /
Every Day	Monday	Tuesday	Wednesday
6:30am			
7:00am			
7:30am			
8:00am			
8:30am			
9:00am			
9:30am			
10:00am			
10:30am			
11:00am			
11:30am			
12:00pm			
12:30pm			
1:00pm			
1:30pm			
2:00pm			
2:30pm			
3:00pm			
3:30pm			
4:00pm			
4:30pm			
5:00pm			
5:30pm			
6:00pm			
7:00pm			

Goals For Today ----

Every Day	Thursday	Friday	Saturday
	Date: /	Date: /	Date: /
6:30am			
7:00am			
7:30am			
8:00am			
8:30am			
9:00am			
9:30am			
10:00am			
10:30am			
11:00am			
11:30am			
12:00pm			
12:30pm			
1:00pm			
1:30pm			
2:00pm			
2:30pm			
3:00pm			
3:30pm			
4:00pm			
4:30pm			
5:00pm			
5:30pm			
6:00pm			
7:00pm			

Goals For Today ----

Every Day	Date: / Monday	Date: / Tuesday	Date: / Wednesday
6:30am			
7:00am			
7:30am			
8:00am			
8:30am			
9:00am			
9:30am			
10:00am			
10:30am			
11:00am			
11:30am			
12:00pm			
12:30pm			
1:00pm			
1:30pm			
2:00pm			
2:30pm			
3:00pm			
3:30pm			
4:00pm			
4:30pm			
5:00pm			
5:30pm			
6:00pm			
7:00pm			

Goals For Today ----

	Date: /	Date: /	Date: /
Every Day	**Thursday**	**Friday**	**Saturday**
6:30am ----------			
7:00am ----------			
7:30am ----------			
8:00am ----------			
8:30am ----------			
9:00am ----------			
9:30am ----------			
10:00am ----------			
10:30am ----------			
11:00am ----------			
11:30am ----------			
12:00pm ----------			
12:30pm ----------			
1:00pm ----------			
1:30pm ----------			
2:00pm ----------			
2:30pm ----------			
3:00pm ----------			
3:30pm ----------			
4:00pm ----------			
4:30pm ----------			
5:00pm ----------			
5:30pm ----------			
6:00pm ----------			
7:00pm ----------			

Goals For Today ----

Every Day	Monday	Tuesday	Wednesday
	Date: /	Date: /	Date: /
6:30am			
7:00am			
7:30am			
8:00am			
8:30am			
9:00am			
9:30am			
10:00am			
10:30am			
11:00am			
11:30am			
12:00pm			
12:30pm			
1:00pm			
1:30pm			
2:00pm			
2:30pm			
3:00pm			
3:30pm			
4:00pm			
4:30pm			
5:00pm			
5:30pm			
6:00pm			
7:00pm			

Goals For Today ----

Every Day	Thursday	Friday	Saturday
	Date: /	Date: /	Date: /
6:30am			
7:00am			
7:30am			
8:00am			
8:30am			
9:00am			
9:30am			
10:00am			
10:30am			
11:00am			
11:30am			
12:00pm			
12:30pm			
1:00pm			
1:30pm			
2:00pm			
2:30pm			
3:00pm			
3:30pm			
4:00pm			
4:30pm			
5:00pm			
5:30pm			
6:00pm			
7:00pm			

Goals For Today ----

Every Day	Monday	Tuesday	Wednesday
	Date: /	Date: /	Date: /
6:30am			
7:00am			
7:30am			
8:00am			
8:30am			
9:00am			
9:30am			
10:00am			
10:30am			
11:00am			
11:30am			
12:00pm			
12:30pm			
1:00pm			
1:30pm			
2:00pm			
2:30pm			
3:00pm			
3:30pm			
4:00pm			
4:30pm			
5:00pm			
5:30pm			
6:00pm			
7:00pm			
Goals For Today ----			

Every Day	Thursday	Friday	Saturday
	Date: /	Date: /	Date: /
6:30am ----------			
7:00am ----------			
7:30am ----------			
8:00am ----------			
8:30am ----------			
9:00am ----------			
9:30am ----------			
10:00am ---------			
10:30am ---------			
11:00am ---------			
11:30am ---------			
12:00pm ---------			
12:30pm			
1:00pm ----------			
1:30pm ----------			
2:00pm ----------			
2:30pm ----------			
3:00pm ----------			
3:30pm ----------			
4:00pm ----------			
4:30pm ----------			
5:00pm ----------			
5:30pm ----------			
6:00pm ----------			
7:00pm ----------			

Goals For Today -----

	Date: /	Date: /	Date: /
Every Day	**Monday**	**Tuesday**	**Wednesday**
6:30am --------			
7:00am --------			
7:30am --------			
8:00am --------			
8:30am			
9:00am --------			
9:30am --------			
10:00am --------			
10:30am			
11:00am --------			
11:30am --------			
12:00pm --------			
12:30pm			
1:00pm --------			
1:30pm			
2:00pm --------			
2:30pm			
3:00pm --------			
3:30pm --------			
4:00pm --------			
4:30pm			
5:00pm --------			
5:30pm --------			
6:00pm --------			
7:00pm --------			

Goals For Today ----

Every Day	Thursday	Friday	Saturday
	Date: /	Date: /	Date: /
6:30am ----------			
7:00am ----------			
7:30am			
8:00am ----------			
8:30am			
9:00am ----------			
9:30am ----------			
10:00am ----------			
10:30am ----------			
11:00am ----------			
11:30am ----------			
12:00pm ----------			
12:30pm			
1:00pm ----------			
1:30pm ----------			
2:00pm ----------			
2:30pm			
3:00pm ----------			
3:30pm ----------			
4:00pm ----------			
4:30pm			
5:00pm ----------			
5:30pm ----------			
6:00pm ----------			
7:00pm ----------			

Goals For Today ----

| | Date: / | Date: / | Date: / |
Every Day	Monday	Tuesday	Wednesday
6:30am			
7:00am			
7:30am			
8:00am			
8:30am			
9:00am			
9:30am			
10:00am			
10:30am			
11:00am			
11:30am			
12:00pm			
12:30pm			
1:00pm			
1:30pm			
2:00pm			
2:30pm			
3:00pm			
3:30pm			
4:00pm			
4:30pm			
5:00pm			
5:30pm			
6:00pm			
7:00pm			

Goals For Today ----

Every Day	Thursday	Friday	Saturday
	Date: /	Date: /	Date: /
6:30am ----------			
7:00am ----------			
7:30am ----------			
8:00am ----------			
8:30am ----------			
9:00am ----------			
9:30am ----------			
10:00am ----------			
10:30am ----------			
11:00am ----------			
11:30am ----------			
12:00pm ----------			
12:30pm ----------			
1:00pm ----------			
1:30pm ----------			
2:00pm ----------			
2:30pm ----------			
3:00pm ----------			
3:30pm ----------			
4:00pm ----------			
4:30pm ----------			
5:00pm ----------			
5:30pm ----------			
6:00pm ----------			
7:00pm ----------			

Goals For Today ----